LONE PINE

Siddhartha Menon has worked in various capacities with schools run by the Krishnamurti Foundation India, for more than thirty years. He is an alum of one of these schools and went on to study English Literature at Delhi University. It was while working at a small rural school near Uttarkashi in the late 1990s that he began to write poetry more seriously, and his first book *Woodpecker* (Sahitya Akademi, 2010) collects poems from this period. Subsequently he has published four further collections. His poems have appeared in various journals and in the following anthologies: *Both Sides of the Sky: Post-Independence Indian Poetry in English, These My Words: The Penguin Book of Indian Poetry* and *Future Library: Contemporary Indian Writing*. He is currently based in Bengaluru.

LONE PINE

Siddhartha Menon

hachette INDIA

First published in India in 2025 by Hachette India
(Registered name: Hachette Book Publishing India Pvt. Ltd)
An Hachette UK Company
www.hachetteindia.com

1

Paperback ISBN 978-93-5731-766-5
eBook ISBN 978-93-5731-860-0

Hachette Book Publishing India Pvt. Ltd
4th/5th Floors, Corporate Centre,
Plot No. 94, Sector 44, Gurugram 122003, India

Typeset in Change 11/14.5
by Mukul

Printed and bound in India by
Manipal Technologies Limited

MIX
Paper | Supporting responsible forestry
FSC™ C043100

to you who read this book in whole or in part
or acquire a copy with noble intent
this book is unreservedly
and with thanks
dedicated

Great Pan is not dead;
he simply emigrated to India.
Here, the gods roam freely,
disguised as snakes or monkeys;
every tree is sacred and it is a sin to be rude to a book.

Sujata Bhatt 'A Different History'

If you are not interested in what I have to say,
Let my words fall anyway, like mermaids' voices
In the background, hushing you, but not saying
Anything you may understand. We are here to stay,
You and I, all day and days until the night closes
My song, and your unhearing.

Vijay Nambisan 'Calypso To Odysseus'

Contents

I. Settings

II. Stirrings

III. Bearings

Settings

Lone Pine

A mountain pine in the plains.
How did it come in this
unfrequented alley? How does it
survive so out of place?
It towers gawkily
above the rear of the building.

Walk past it every morning
to touch its toughness. Its needles
are dropping always. They are
the sponginess you tread.
A few are caught in the bark's
rigid flakes. Gently
prise them out. Release them
to fall where they belong.

They cover dust and flatness
with the scent of resin slopes.

That arrival: a return.
The car with shut windows
had wound through a pine forest.
At last you stood on a ridge
in the blue forgotten air
through which the great trees
were a dry redolence.

It seemed that this was it:
belonging. Home was this.

But the pines kept murmuring
something else. You are
a guest wherever you are:

home is out of place.

Eucalyptus

They are culpable
of drawing the water there is to great lengths.
Some say that being outsiders
they should not remain.
Others say that an outsider is God.

Look at this one: its pared-to-the-bone glow
that sets it apart from the dark
profusion of natives all around.
It is the first to be lit
its lean intensity to draw the sun

ray by ray to this native earth.

The Lesson

Maybe this tree was never meant to be here.
No one remembers how it came.
A short-lived evening dust-storm
has collapsed its major bough
exposed a cavern at the base
with termite residues. Chunks of yellow wood
as fresh as they are jagged:
the small marauders hadn't blunted them.
How sturdily the tree had kept from view
the stealthy eating from inside.
It towered over this patch of the earth
as it had to. It was a stable empire.

Its towering is done. What is left
is for a tree to be imagined as it once was
for us to receive in its place the sun.
Trace the thews of the fallen arm
the bumps and hollows of time's artistry
on fallen wood. Get as close as you wish.
Step over it where it has come to earth –
this is your transgressive power
as one of the living. But even in decline
it leaves a mark. It is here to stay
as a monumental lesson.
Regret has so little to do with it.

Confluence

1. Sun

You saw it large
as it came into a roundness
and changed unendingly the colours

pushed aside by oars.

In your snapshot
it has come smaller than a bird
whose circling is held interminably

in colours whose change has ended.

2. Stars

See the lights on the water.
No they are not straying reflections
of templed streets.

Platters of lamps
floated out upriver
on a lost current

come this far flickering
without being dimmed:
a flotilla of riverine stars.

3. Moon

The biggest full moon of the year
when kheer is placed on the roof
to be touched by it.
The night afterwards
the river is sheathed by the overfed moon
crumbling silently
with all that heavy sweetness.
A train sounds the bridge invisibly.
You sense the shore-hungry boat
sidling past. An oar
flashes petitions to the moon.

4. Boy

Across the water and in front
of the darkening facade of steps
that rise to heaven between the shadows

orange flares are bunched like potted plants.
Their smoke overcasts the stained tiers.

You cannot smell the char of incense
nor at this distance hear
the hiss of flames the crack of a skull
the lap of petalled water on boats.

And on this shore of the fallen river
a boy plays in the white sand
shaping it as he wills
as his father watches and the other shore
dwindles. The flares begin
to be carried in black water.

River Mornings

1. Colours

Look down there at the blue umbrella
sticking up with its white florals
from the small brown boat
that hugs the bank of the grey
and rained-on river.

The wind pushes wavelets ahead of the flow.
The furrows take on every hue
that the current tunnels beneath.

Another boat is being muscled
against the surge by a man in a black t-shirt.

For a moment he rests his oars
then pulls past the umbrella
and past a rain-darkened peacock
that stands on the motley debris
left by a river that might be green or silver.

It might be anything.
Unlike on mornings that a saffron glaze
becomes a hard glitter.

2. Stylus

At this time the river plays you nothing.
Lights are strung across its black sheen.

The bridge is a train's horn and rumble.
The ashram bell is hitting what notes it can.

The first ray is lowered deftly.
It cleanly picks up embedded colours

skips the ashram and muffles the bridge.
Dust is hardening in grooves.

3. Iron

The sun is so anaemic you wonder
how it will get through a long day.

Sky and water are lead.

Watch the sun tightening
until you can only avert your eyes.

But it will regain colour.

Come back to it in wonder then:
see it flushed with the molten iron

that sinks it into the trees.

4. The Sun In Disguise

Streaked across and florid the sun
as if it were Jupiter
set to score with a thunderbolt.

On the river it leaves a gash
into which a thin boat is edged penitentially
against a current

that drives underneath
wind-ruffled surfaces. The sun
melted water the sun draws the wind

there is nothing the sun has nothing to do with
so when it comes as a mere planet
it fools nobody.

Now the time to wade
and in prescribed directions to scoop water
for light to slip through fingers.

5. Hologram

And mornings when blank river
fuses into far shore
shore to sky

so the boat being drawn slowly
across the grey absence
is on all of these

or none of them
a thing wholly of light
a dark shimmer

6. Ignoring The Evidence

Today the river lies low and smelly
but vastly picturesque as always
so if you ignored the high watermarks
a lore of epic cleansing would come to mind.

Today you hear a mountain torrent.
Ignore the slime that comes with it
and you have a foaming cataract
discharged on high for sacred waters to rise.

7. Bluster And The River

The wind let loose by the saffron sun
is doing all it can
to blow the river off its course
and sway the trees that slant at the edge.

And look – it is succeeding.
The colour-dazzled surface
is being driven helter-skelter
as the trees can only duck their heads.

The stain on the water does not run deep.
The river is an undertow
whose destination is as safe
as the anchoring of trees.

8. Battleground

A drowned-earth retreat: the water
leaves unpretty sludge.
Fence posts reappear aslant
with barbed wires collapsing.

Some trees have stood firm
their trunks held down by the corpses
of face-down paper plates and ripped
entrails of plastic.

But look: behind the foliage
a brightening has begun.
Watch how the concealed river
ambushes the sun.

9. Ol’ Man River

The flanks of the brown river
beneath the massed and shadowless clouds
fan out and slide into the shore.

Midstream the water is patchy
but looks immune as armoured cars
to being diverted by myths on the side.

The river is not an old man.
Nor has it ever been the Mother
no matter the evening pieties on show.

It is young blood obeying old commands
to just keep rollin’ along.
It bundles silt towards an ocean.

10. Hanamichi

He stands on a low platform
that slants gradually into the water.
All in white he faces the river
and has it lapping on either side.

His shoes must be getting wet.
His hands are moving theatrically
as if he were on the flower passage
to an underwater stage.

He may have risen through a trapdoor.
His only company is the pigeons
to whom he is throwing crumbs.
They are not importunate.

They know what they can expect
as if they have played at every staging
of an act that ends like all the world
but signifies something.

Keeping Time

Three peahens in the scrub
step daintily together while three
exuberant dogs dash to the water's edge
followed discreetly by a fourth
who when he reaches his mates
allows his white tail a single wag.
The peahens turn up their noses
at the gushing sewer slowed by the river
but the dogs have their noses down
where earth gives way to water
and bare-bodied men strung out
are tugging at a net
to which a boat just out is tethered.
They pull, relax and pull again.
Now they release their hold
and two of them wade in
towards the boat that turns unhurriedly
on the grey vastness
as if preparing to merge with it.
It is the women
who bring sharp tones to this confluence
in veils blue and orange.
They try to raise the tempo
through voice and gesture. Nothing
will slow them down but they
will find it hard to speed things up.

Breathing

The winter sun is a big draw:
it inspires the oarsman

who is rowing at ease
against the almost stagnant river.

You see him as blue and facing him
a smaller figure in red.

As he leans to lift and skim the oars
you inhale with him

then let go slowly to his massive
furrowing of water.

Its sound does not carry
nor the voices red and blue.

They go for the going sun
the breath releasing them yours.

Fog

1. What It Does

Each thing slow
to centre-stage
is swiftly whited out

Around a dim sapling
that wire mesh

stark and in its way
striking

2. Naming

Red flowers stare above the path
the petals scentless:
it is the river seeping in

Exposed all night flowers
in your face: no name

"Flower" will have to do
like "fog"

3. The Large Picture

You do not see the woods
but see one by one the trees
as itinerant shadows

They stand shapely
in less than three dimensions

You do not know leaf
from twig

4. The Temple-Tree

This is not a cat's-foot fog
Before dawn you heard it
occupy this place

It has left benches stained
and earth darkened

How the stripped temple-tree
clutches

A Cool Morning In Summer

Leaves are driven right up to the door.

Clouds positioned ahead of time:
who would say it is peak summer?

Coolness out of time: will it prove costly

the summer flowers wither early
the birds that should be going stay?

Leaves

1. Pausing

One dark leaf is a midair blot
above the wicket gate.
What keeps it there against the tended

wilderness? It seems
to be attached to no strings.
It is a long pause.

Beyond it a speckled bird
is twittering on and off.
The leaf is a fall

broken. An absence caught
so it does not spread. Erasure
will not leave a mark.

2. Listening

The leaves above the scudding river
are an intimate language. How
understand the fire-fed workings of a heart?

The leaves have so much going on
so little time. The wind fans their urgency
knocks defectives down.

Pores are being cranked open
furnaces stoked inside.
Exchanges overseen by the wind are never halted.

Even in stillness the leaves are heard.
What of understanding? Begin to eavesdrop
on work that pulses hiddenly.

Not Leaves

It is the tenth day already:
before you know it the twentieth.
Ten more and a month is out of reach.

Clusters on a branch above the terrace.
Yesterday they were wondered at
today no end to them.

Small birds detach a few
that dwindle into the paving.
Days that went almost unnoticed.

One you pick up so like the others
cracks. Your palm is left
with a spill of two black seeds.

Orange Flowers

These flowers on the hedge
appear as if they are
embarrassed by the allure

of their orangeness.
The way they dip behind leaves
you would think them coy.

But it also appears that they
are not wholly averse
to being noticed – the shortlived

immodest twits that they are.

Moonflower

It must be a paler version of a sunflower.
It must be a follower through the night.
As it cranes its neck to the moon it segues
from orange smoulder to loud white

and back as the moon drops into trees.
Its flowering is paused when the sun appears.
Its petals that fade in patches begin
by high noon to close on silence.

Too changeable to try and spread
its scents dwindle as you come near.
Its baby softness must be a cover:
if you must pluck it protect your hands.

Moon Insect

Behind the insect is half a moon.
The dim sky lies between them.
How if they could touch!

The moon as always has its place.
It will not be drawn
by the earth's simple feelers.

But it does not repel either.
Thus on hidden strings to a leaf
an insect's perkiness.

Amaltas

It startles you each time:
so much yellow exquisiteness
hanging over the path.

But so unpretty
the torso flaked and mottled
like skin with old burns.

It is as if a blacksmith
were dripping lines of poetry.
You may watch

one by one a twirl
a tie broken.
Here they lie on the bricks.

You need to be iron-hearted
to take them in your stride
no other way.

Pick one up.
It is so delicately realized
that it had to land just so.

But what about this one
that lies unopened
like a casket? Why?

Its parts folded in and perfect
will never be exposed:
unheard, unwritten.

Semal

It catches you through dust and motorbikes.

Rearing above the slope in the lane
offset by the spring-blue sky
a pale trunk with branches bare
except for the high clustering: orange

not the ruddiness you see elsewhere.
Beautiful sure but bleached
so you wonder if in the kingdom of trees
this is the imperfection

of words where beauty is a falling short.

The Pond

Tightly circumscribed
by red garden tiles
on them spreadeagled in plaster

effigies of birds.
The stilled and dark water
floats enormous leaves.

Spectral a flower rises
slightly askew on the stem
that is too spindly for it.

A large black hump with etched
hexagons is a turtle
whose head half-submerged

is tilted raffishly
a white knob for an eye
a frozen hint of a grin.

Tableau. A flicker. Something
sleek and easy slid in
soundless and rippleless.

What? You peer. You find
nothing that isn't held.
Whatever enters here

must cease. Reflections of trees
disguise the drowned stems
that sway skeletally.

One of the leaves has stretched
onto the tiles. No space
between captive leaves

for the outsized frog at the edge
come like crazy alive
to effect a haiku entry.

Stirrings

Waking

1. The Horn

You are again awake
when you should not be. There is no way back.
You do not know how long it has been
since the last dream let go.

You wish you were held again.

What snares you now is the call
of wagons trundling over and out of the bridge.
It should be nothing to you:
not a signal nor an alarm

but you are pulled along.

2. Trio

A foghorn
a solitary star
you hear one and
do not see the other
but every time you wake
they come back to you
inseparable and now
you fear their loss
to each other
to you

3. Summer Bird

At 3 a.m. you hear it.

You say this means winter is over
and the night is over
for you. But you re-enter your dreams.
So you may be wrong about winter too.

You wake again to hear it first thing.

Has it been going all this while?
It had dropped out of sound in autumn
and almost out of mind.
Now it is unwavering. You say

winter dreamlike has gone.

Hard to say for how long.

4. Paralytic

things / that can't move / learn to see

Louise Glück 'The Hawthorn Tree'

After a night's rain you dream of sleep.
Something must end this stillness.

Clothes on the terrace can only drip.
The trees are too full to move.

You are empty but held. Thinking
never gave up on you through the night.

Your eyes are heavy but you are learning
to see. Among thorns the berries.

5. Night And Day

All night you saw more clearly
how things were going to be.

The hours quickly went by.
The jackals raised their voices
then the peacocks.

Your mind was a cutting edge.
Then daylight yawned.

Seeing Becomes A Poem

It began on the walkway through the scrub.
Dawn was on the other side of trees.
A coucal marked time invisibly.
A rustling of leaves turned your head.
They saw you when you saw them.
Three jackals paused what they were doing.
The rustling ceased.
Your footsteps died.
Beyond the jackals a nilgai stopped.
It turned its head towards you.
Eyes were trained on you.
Yours were not so steady.
The thin trees cast no shadows.
The coucal was going deep.
Seeing had fixed you on a tightrope.
Something had to give.
The jackals went about their business.
The nilgai turned away.
A balance slipped out of your hands.
You landed on a pile of words.
Brush them off carefully.
They are tattered almost poetic.
Dawn is all over the place.
Nothing is so becoming.

Time For Nothing

The oval amphitheatre is silent.
Trees all round the tiers
lean inwards
as if to watch nothing take place.

The steps are covered in dry leaves
from which a dog lifts its ears
to your untimely arrival.
It says nothing.

Not so the morning birds:
their tongues are wagged as always.
They leave nothing unremarked
not even silence.

Aubade

Only you are on the brick path.
Puddles bring out the unevenness
where it skirts the amphitheatre
whose floor is a sheath of brown water.

Fat drops land on your head.
The trees are bending more than usual.
There are limits to what they will carry
and they are dark with it.

But the sky was changing
so fast: you were in a floodlight
silent around you the trees
beneath a freshly laundered shroud.

Running Past

You round a corner
to see a path of embedded bricks
stretching away from the sun that is rising
onto the opened ground.
Distantly on the path is a bundle.
As you near you see it is a man
sitting cross legged
his back to the sun and to you.
His head is bowed
to your rapid approach
on a track that was only his
to do anything with.
Possessing it has been too much for him.
Hunched in the middle of nowhere
is he expecting his shoulders
to be jolted upright?
Does he spy intent
in the shadow mirror ahead of him?
Will he look up when it is crossed
by yours? Will he then
with self-possession intact
watch all the way
your bright and diminishing back?

Joggers

You approach the broad whiteness.
A jogger crosses you ahead
and both of you wave
uncertainly through the lingering fog.
Then another and now a third.
They are well protected
in dark sleeves and tights and gloves
with things pulled over their ears.
Swallowed up now
they must be somewhere on the track
for there is nowhere else to go.
You wait behind a black tree
for them to come around again
their reappearance on the curve
delivered by fog for a snapshot where they
offset the tree's stillness
with theirs. Now you hear
a patter like things let loose by the trees
and now they are going past
their breaths condensing
as they set off on another round.
They fade into the far curve
and the field again lies emptied.
Somewhere between you

and the canopy emerging above the fog
in that low vastness somewhere
is a train of exhalations
simple words being chuffed
to another round of the sun.

Rubber Bands

There he goes in a blue t-shirt
with the white lid of a yellow water bottle
poking out of a brown cloth bag.
All those colours on him
and time enough to stroll beneath the trees:

is his thinking full of colour
to embellish what he does?
He was used to going places.
Can he now keep up with his thoughts?

The years tug at you
not with locomotive smoothness
but as a rubber band
a stretch here or a stretch
there. Now and then a stinging rebound.
You to hold things together
while being thinned to breaking point.

He has not snapped. Stiffening he goes
with time on his hands and at his heels.

Puncture

Steadiness is getting harder.
You are almost down to the rims.

Turn memories through your fingers
inch-wise in a shallow bowl

for telltale bubbles to appear.

To watch is a kind of buoyancy.

Phone Photographer

The last sky of yesterday
the first of today
trees jagging into what light there is.

No telling which is which
without captions. No labels

suffice for skies in transit.
Call the night that fell between them
a day.

The Quilt

It wraps your bone-chill in padding.
It is a soft turbine
that generates dreams.

You have to be acquiescent.
You have no means to stanch the endless
replenishment:

dreams cavorting like paper boats
in a broken gutter.
The quilt thaws the marrow

a child is being unfrozen in sleep.

Writing In Winter

This is the cold of swollen fingers
and branches carved by the mist.

Night sounds stay on for longer now
but they are muffled.

The desk shows no sign of a thaw:
entrust it with all you carry.

Let the pen do its thing
scoring here and there as fingers skid.

Prickly Heat

On days of prickly heat
poetry stays away.
On days of poetry
prickly heat lies low.

There must be a lesson in their
not coming together.

Some untruth as well.

For who would resist a poem's
itch?

Words In Season

Already the summer night is ending.
A crow breaks the stillness.
This you expand to "Only a crow..." etc.
and watch the leaf-fall of truth.

Sweep this too aside for "Only this crow
to break the morning stillness"
to ape the plenitude of
"Season of mists and mellow fruitfulness".

Your words have a wintry stomp.
Come back to a crow breaking
a stillness and find that it has its footfall too.
Spring is in your feet.

A Poem For Lunch

You read a poem aloud
to a bemused class.

A recollection of boy
and mother in quiet

bending heads over
a kitchen task.

The moment her breath
is said to be in his

a smile awakens a face.
A pair of eyes lit up

lights the room
whets an appetite.

Teenagers

They think the whole world is in their hands.
He calls for you to wait.
You turn around. He is taking his time.
He is carrying something. Both hands.
Please walk with me, he says,
I need to take it home, and the dogs...
He has reached you. Cradled
on large leaves is a throbbing bird.
Greenish, greyish, injured.
You want to look away.
What happened to it, you ask.
A scavenger attacked it, he explains,
because they also need to eat.
(Does he mean a *predator*?
But one is sometimes the other
and this is not the time to ask or correct.)
His house is near and you see no dog.
You were about to go in the other direction.
Just keep walking, you say,
nothing will happen. He nods.
He starts off. You watch from behind.
I am with you, you call,
as if you were an invisible god.
A dog appears on the other side of a hedge
and trots alongside them with intent.
You go after and chase it off.
Now you walk with him.

What will you do with it?
He names precisely the medicinal drops
the food and the number of days
for it to heal.
You have come to a junction of paths
where his house is straight ahead
lit by the early sun.
You turn around.
You take a flower-strewn path
whose dogs regard you casually.
They also need to eat.
Friend to scavengers
and no enemy to dogs
he's got everything in his hands.

After The Peacock

All in white the three boys
are chasing after something
in the afternoon shade of the banyan tree.
Wheeling and calling out
their arms flailing
and one of them barefoot they
are ready for the kill.
They think they are closing in.

Yet there it goes
clumsy but resplendent.
It skims the ground with everything outstretched
then lifts and banks to the nearest roof.
That is its usual spot.

Restored to eminence
it commands the entrance with a jaundiced eye
and sounds a mournful note
to no one in particular.
That is where at odd times
it spreads its tail
to make sure it still can get it up.
For it is old
dysfunction looms.
Where it was will be a space.

The boys have had their run
at it. Their jeers
unshade the promise of things to come.

Uncommon Babbler

A stir. Two boys are on their feet
food forgotten
transfixed by something high behind you.
Others are looking too.
A spoon is suspended between plate and mouth.
There are calls for the ceiling fans to be turned off.
Someone gets to the switchboard
and the fans begin slowly to fall silent.
Hall-wide a prick of apprehension:
a bird. A silent babbler
has blundered in through the great doors
is trying in haphazard bursts of flight and pause
the meshed ventilators above the windows.
In its flight paths the deadly blades are still revolving.
Somehow it misses them.
You would rather sweat
than have blood and brokenness to contend with.
It has come to the vent nearest to you.
Its eye is staring its voice is lost
it turns this way then that.
Everyone is watching.

Tea

He hugs his tumbler of tea.
It is the most precious thing.
He stands beneath a dripping tree
where those who still serve
have served him.

They are at their posts again.
He was here as usual early
and was given tea.
Now that his service is over why
does he exist?

Scuffed shoes and shapeless pants
that he has to pull up
full sleeves almost empty
with bones. But his tumbler
has just been filled.

Taking Off

1. Shortcut

You take the shortcut across the lawn's
relentless night-shadows. You notice
as you come near the lamp-post end
a smallness on the path.
Why does it not move at your approach?
You pass it and stop to look.
An owlet! Three feet from you
and standing on the hardened earth
but bent slightly backward
to see you unwinkingly the better.
You look at one another.
It begins to sway its head from side to side
a rocking doll a stuffed cobra
an owlet. You are mesmerized.
It is too but why?
You are not swaying before it
and it must have seen others pass this way.
Is it putting on a show
so you know what it can do on this earth?
Or only to convey
that you have trespassed
and should have taken the long way round?
But is it injured? Grounded
when it must have a tree to which it belongs.

You take a step towards it
and it stops its swaying.
A squeak – or was it a squawk? –
then a flying low away from you
the quickest route taken
to a space untouched by light
by shadows by you.

2. Triangle

With crest pricked the bulbul on a banister
steep stairs going down to the river
looks towards you.

The light is dim. You recognize
by its sharp angles
on the post opposite the bulbul's a robin.
An arm's length from one another
they are isosceles to your peering vertex.
No constellation this:

not here to keep an equidistance
or tow you flatly across a void.
Off in four dimensions

they are songs above the river.

3. You Are And It is

It lands right in front of you.
You are no perch
no shelter for it yet here unmoving
it is and you are. It blends
into the dampened earth.
A moment takes time to pass. Another
your eye adjusting
discloses a white streak.
It stays grounded for the third
moment. Then a chirr
onto a branch just out of your reach.
There it is for the time being
just as here you are
and the earth unmoved is.

The Conch

A bicycle creak heralds the milkman.
So loud he needn't call
to your neighbour to bring him her can.

And yet below her window he does.
And she calls back
before padding down the stairs to him.

Their calling is not unlike
the sounding of the conch next door at dawn.
Again at dusk.

To her a summons. To you
intimations of things you have passed
passing you.

The Chant

The chant comes over the trees
to the dark playground. Your jog

began heavy footed
but things are lightening.

Your track is hardened earth
you pad to a rhythm, crunch

fallen seed-pods. The chant
comes to you in gusts.

You take the curve again
to follow footsteps: yours.

The chant carries the sun's
circuit, your breath, a pulse.

The Griper At The Gates Of Dawn

Grouching across the river
is a sleep-laced voice
offset by the temple bells
that hasten to strike the daylight in.
He is gruffly melancholic
his cadence faltering
the tune a simple rise and fall
that is at times broken
by a very low note or a high
or a sudden speeding up for night's exit.
At times too by a prosy exhortation
whose words are indistinct.
The message is in the sound.

He sounds too world-weary
and there are too many uneven pauses
for this to be a recording.
Yet if you rise with the last darkness
the voice is here
and you will have to listen.
It seems each time to query
the turns you have taken all along.
But the questioning ends abruptly
and listening gives way to the sun.

You tell yourself you will seek him out
in the maze above the ghats.
Which gate ajar is his?
Or is he out on the streets
holding a lantern to every face?
You visualize an all-seeing man
who will ask you to not block the light
but who sees you best unlit.

Teens On Shravan Monday

So many of them barefoot and merry
striding through the unholy muck
on the ghats at dawn.
It isn't that the new dustbins have overflowed:
they are mere appendages
to a smart city whose time has been coming
since the inception of time.
More of the boys are in the murky water
splashing within red barriers
that keep them from colliding with boats
or being carried off.
Not that such things are to be feared:
the boats are slow
these waters can only drown misdeeds
and this is an auspicious month
with fasts to be observed
precociously. What of hunger? Nothing
requires smart phones to be given up.
Here is music and there are selfies
arms resting on shoulders
nineteen to the dozen strong.

Literary Event

Yet if it does not seem a moment's thought,
Our stitching and unstitching has been naught.
W.B. Yeats 'Adam's Curse'

I

The last embers of daylight... enter
the terrace of the would-be heritage hotel
whose lanterns keep the river hidden.
There she is – on a bench
conversing with the other two
her back to you but recognizable
by her hair that is let straight down
just as in the photo.
Go over and introduce yourself? No
this is no place for butting in.
The night has come in early
and there will be time and quietness.

II

A faintly awkward moment on this terrace
with the black river chuckling behind:
three local men (the "moderators")
three foreign women (two novelists, a poet)
are lined up to be introduced.
Strangers are faced together to share

a chancy intimacy.
Nine handshakes.
A peeling off in pairs with some
getting-to-know to be done quickly
before the following night's business.
The women have come to an unknown place:
will their translated words survive the distance?
The men do not know their writers' work.
They hadn't known their names
until the invitation. Tomorrow
an audience is to be faced.

III

Yours is the poet which is to say
you are the poet's. She seems a little jittery too
but maybe her gesticulations
at odds with the hard-to-hear voice
are just her way and she is actually
as much at ease as anyone ever is.
Red lips white dress a lilting
emphasis with eyes dark and flickering.
You interrupt each other's questions
and answer simultaneously
then settle into a rhythm of listening
and not uncomfortable silences.
The lights are subdued and to talk poetry
would not be seen as idle here.
You say you will swap your books.
Yours will have to wait till tomorrow

but before leaving she remembers hers
and fishes out from a brown handbag
the slim collection whose cover you've seen online.

IV

Intermittently next day you read. The even
pages are in her language of choice, the odd
draw you in and keep you out
in the language that you share.
You do not catch her voice always
but recognize at times a soundscape, a calling
inside the earth's dark rivers.
Perhaps this is a way you too will go
though it leads to the edge of a northern sea.
In the afternoon some verses rise
like islands revealed by a falling tide.
You linger as if you now know what it is
to be local in a foreign land.

V

Evening again. Time to set out. But what
to write in the pair of books you'll give her?
Write anything at all? Yes
but how to not sound familiar
without a stiffness you do not feel?
And write the same words in both? Eventually
that is what you do: a scrawl
that looks a moment's thought the first time.

But the second? You tell yourself
she will receive your edgy reticence
as a kind of poet-to-poet thing.

VI

Together at dinner with two convivial hosts
the conversation brings to light
kinships in the written word.
But you should be talking less
of things that are her birthright
and listening instead to that hesitant voice.
You keep your end of the exchange
and with the table cleared
watch her frown of concentration
as she inscribes with a careful hand
and at your request the book she had given you.
She translates the words that she has put in brackets:
a poet entrusting you with poetry.

VII

You sit together under the white canopy
in the first row of white-draped chairs
as if you were early to a reception.
People begin to file in.
The invisible river is almost at the door
three (or is it four?) flights below this terrace.
Her voice seems softer as the time draws near.
She says that her brother had quipped

when she began to teach
that her students would learn to lip-read at least.
You conspire half in earnest
that after she has done her public reading
rather than engage in literary chat
you will sit companionably in silence.
Words may be a curse
if labour does not make them beautiful.

VIII

The other two go first. In between
you offer her water from your bottle.
She first declines then takes a sip.
An interval is announced for refreshments
and twenty minutes extend to forty
of milling around in a kind of purgatory.
Suddenly the big lights are off
and a spot is on you on simple chairs
backed by a banner. You are
emissaries of verse in the wake of prose
with a table between you for the hand-held mics
and the earthen cups with water. Would silence
not be a salve for a word-hit audience?

IX

She reads alternately. You wonder
about the waters forded in translation
and the things that do not make it.

You sense more clearly than before
that poetry is a mother tongue
whose crossings out and in will stay unfinished.
Now you hear a permeable music
and know it to be an undertow
of watchfulness and moving on.
But how to say this there? She reads
only a little and her voice steadies.
She responds to your public questions
as if they were worth responding to.
She insists you read as well
and feeling like a gatecrasher you do
self-consciously and from a screenshot
in a silenced phone:
artful words on the smell of time.
They are offset by her parting shaft
"how silence improves lipstick"
taken up like a wisp by the rooftop wind
and carried to the invisible river.

X

At almost midnight it ends.
The small crowd begins to disperse
as you are lined in a glare for photographs.
Will they capture at this hour
a whiff that isn't watered by time?
She is to leave the next morning and you
are to make your way along the river
to the other side of the wakeful city.

At 1 AM you empty your backpack.
Around the nozzle of the water bottle
is a thin smear of red
and in the improving silence you hear a voice
no longer so soft but never loud.

The Smell Of Time

for Sundar Sarukkai

He says this might be a good title
for a poem. That poem

a dung pungency just out the window
a first-rain tartness

going the way of poets who cannot
resist a sniff of death.

They have seen colours of infirmity
heard tunes of decay.

But odourless as health their poems
no matter the smell of time.

Shedding

whatever else we might think of the world -
it is astonishing
Wislawa Szymborska 'The Poet and the World'

Leaves so thickly fallen
we do not now know the path
from the wilderness through which it winds.

What is this? How come?

No easing into summer this year:
spring has been swept aside
leaves have had to be junked in a rush.

Always like this?

The river through naked trees
has begun to shed its late glitter.

Like always.

We have begun to shed astonishment.

How come?

Like always.

What You Saw

Three men in a boat as if
three generations.
One a boy really.

This is as much as you tell.
And watching them the joy
that lights you here.

To see with your eyes
or recall what you have seen
is to improvise:

the vastness of the river's
pallor at dawn
the boat like a drifting leaf

with its laid-back trio
who carry time between them.
They trail a net on the surface

as an afterthought.
It spreads but there is nothing
they wish to keep.

Nothing to lose in the current
not even your
watching them or my

trawling for words. For three
seen in a boat
passing then as now.

True East

We have stopped at the edge of the field
to look at the sun just risen.
You hold your compass out. See!
That's not where the sun should be...

so many degrees off the east.
I wish to restitute the sun
declare that the compass must be wrong.
But that would not be true.

Children we love hear us proclaim
that the sun rises in the east
although we know it does not rise.
And now the east is equivocal.

What do the children learn of us?
Our directions are as our love.

Lid Of A Broken Bottle

The just-filled plastic water bottle
slips out of the bag
hits a stone and breaks in two.

A clean divide.
The edges fit together neatly
but their split is final.

The lid is tightly screwed.
The lid is intact
like some misunderstandings.

We skirt attentively the spilt
water.

The Bridge

The day begins with endings.
A message confirms the collapse
of an arched fantasy.
The news of a death belies
another fantastic event:
the union of man and woman.
One of them is weeping
along with a child who knows
as something covered in blankets
is stretchered out. The day
is hazy and began for you
at water's edge. The boats
were tethered on sand. The bridge
was lit like a birthday cake.

The Pine Touch

Time to pause at the foreign pine
caress its bark.

Why are there times you walk right past
and do not see it?

Tonight with words passing us by
eyes are holding on.

Not native to each other
but a thing touched has taken root.

Moving On

If you do not belong here
you belong they say nowhere.
This is where folk arrive
when they think their time is nearing.

Touch this tree as you pass.

Come back to it one more time
on the eve of departure. You are
out of place no more
than the owlet that isn't here.

Shake out your wings and leave.

Bearings

Coconut Man

'This man can't bear our life here and will drown,'
The abbot said, 'unless we help him.'
Seamus Heaney 'Lightenings viii'

If he were to fall he would be broken
though you might not hear him shout.
Where would that leave us?
His feet are bound, the tree between them,
and each time he draws them up
to the weapon dangling at his waist
he looks like a frog poised to leap.
Up and up as if gravity did not exist.
Why is this trunk so tall?
No rigging for him to hold on and rest
no hindering his progress.
And then he is hidden among the fronds.
A crow on a neighbouring mast
watches with its head craned.
A shadow movement: he has made it.
A thwack and another.
A coconut drops and breaks nothing
not even itself
though there is nothing to break its fall.
You hear it thud and roll.
Then more are dropped after it.
Now he is cutting entire fronds
that plummet like severed wings.

Is there a warning sign
that things are falling out of the sky?
He stands exposed.
He looks all round unhurriedly
as if he were a periscope.
Nothing further up here. Your job is over
and what is left is a shinning down.
Lower yourself by stretching bound feet
and drawing your torso after them.
Stretch and draw
between tautness and release
take air and draw and stretch
then pause as if you were nailed.
Touch down. But this is not the end.
Now where a crow once watched
climb back into the life that is yours.
You need no help: the tree's tallness
is where you breathe
and you are tied to elevation.

Road Roller

It reverses rapidly up the mud
to the loud beeping set off by the gear.
It has red lights flashing
and lamps sticking out of the cab like eyes.
Its weight is no impediment
and at this speed it could be a mean machine
worth getting on for the ride.

Look at those
tyres, that streamlined nose, the gleam
of the nameplate, the sign: Volvo.
It goes outside of your window frame
to the cul-de-sac.

The beeping stops
and birdsong is lifted where it had fallen.

Then the window rattles
and the floor begins to quake.
You become the earth's tremor
as the drum is vibrated all the way back down
unhurriedly so there is no mistaking
a power that is all intent.

Anything that is raised is going to be flattened
like it or leave it everything
will have its turn beneath those eyes. A mean
machine. You are in for the ride.

You have to be.

The Excavator

Under the sun the gleaming excavator
is at work on the river bank.
Or is this play?
It swivels back and forth
between the dredged mud and a lorry.

The man in the cabin
drives these rapid arcs that end abruptly
where they need to.
The boom swings a shadow across the earth
and the lorry's bay is filled in no time.

But this maw will have to ply much longer
to make a lasting impression
on the piles of glistening riverbed.
Which is why at dawn the next day
the work goes on.

Or is it play?
To be cocooned with a push-button console
beside the narrowed river
unleash hydraulic power on yourself and the world:
to be a pivot in a larger game.

The boys clambering on the grey heaps
are having such a good time.
From a precipice they slide

they shove each other off
they flounder up and thump their chests.

They are kings of dirt ahead of the sun.
Their colours offset the mud
safe for marionettes
with power at their fingertips
to scoop and carry and dump to their heart's content.

Outsider

Outsiders must learn this river's code.

Today the sun will be shrouded
but the bare bodied men at water's edge
know when it is time.

Nothing can stop their moment.
A conch. They raise water in their palms
and hail the rising they cannot see.

Their voices carry the day.
One of them is doing something expansive
with a cupped flame.

Their call makes light of sludgy steps.
It has gone up through tree and temple
to rouse once-forgiving streets.

This call you remember from story books
was raised in war against infidels.
Now it so inflames piety

outsiders must learn to lie low.

Mosque And Temple

I

Mosque and temple are cheek by jowl
are kindred spirits are
thick as thieves.
Their nearness is a dirty joke.
The swollen domes
evade the grasp of newly anointed walls
though the walls are manly
and the domes tautly nippled.

II

Skintight khakis:
boredom finds release in commandeered tea
and squirts of bloodlike spittle.
No holding back
but iron barriers at every turn
ensure openings are closed.
The exemplary hold on scratchy groins
delays satisfaction.

III

Where history is a hooker
bloodlust finds an outlet.
Barriers cannot contain it.

Not much space to do it. Nor for burial.
But the gullies can take fire.
Wood is stockpiled
beside the big-time myth-bending river.
Domes begin to sag.

Again That Wretched "Dreck"

and they saw no longer the battlefield
Vivek Narayanan *After*

I mean the truth untold,
The pity of war, the pity war distilled
Wilfred Own 'Strange Meeting'

No escaping this word.
It grates finely as if it almost carried
all our histories of friendly fire.

Whether to call it wretched
like calling fresh water sweet or war
a pity: the true word sounds itself.

We are led in strange unseeingness
to bayonets being piled
onto the wordless people they ended.

We pause to intone to the hollowed earth
You were the enemy I killed
my friend. Words are almost dreck.

Concert

If music be the food of love, play on.
William Shakespeare *Twelfth Night* I.i

1. Hall

The river catches the last light of day.
You cross the road and mount the broad stairs
follow directions to the correct portal
of this unruined acropolis.
Red carpets and long chandeliered hallways.
At the box office your stacked ticket is retrieved
(if you show "proof of identity").
It comes enveloped and is bestowed on you
like a birth certificate. With it in hand
you are ushered up staircases
by liveried survivors stationed at every turn.
Kind and smiling one of them
guides you through a door with a gilded knob
to the very chair you had envisaged
online all those months ago.
The view is good. From your balcony
you see a precious world.
You do not know if you belong. But you
are certified in place on time
to hear a cacophony of tuning and sounding.
How adept they are at dissonance.
Somewhere a bell and the hall-lights dim

for silence to descend.
Now we are ready to begin.
This river once was a frontier of war
where something apparently was settled.
Events these many months
remind us that there is always more
settling of scores, more rendering
ticketless homeless limbless
less. Out-of-syncness is a threat.
But here disparate noises are harmonized.
The hall allows us to forget
despite our tiered vantage points
that certificates of dying
are not for everyone. Forget too
in music's dying fall
the true acoustics of revenge.

2. Conductor

Iron-haired his back is towards you.
After his walk through the violinists
after the profound bow to his audience
two staged handshakes and an expansive gesture
to the rest of his crew
after the single step up and a moment's pause
he has been in silent motion all through.
Some of his cues are portentous
some almost imperceptible
but he mimetically is running the show.
A railing ensures he will not stray to the edge

though he does not look the straying type.
He turns his pages without looking at them
as if they were an irrelevance.
And maybe now they are: all of
conflict and resolution
is knots unravelling from his tidied brain
to the point of his little wand.
How he brings off in silence
a skewering of untidiness. How they all
are his to a cinder.

3. Harps

Even before they are sounded
look: they stand like the sides of a battle chariot
descended from antiquity.

Like words before they are sounded
that carry barbs. Bare armed the women pluck:
fingers speak in curlicues.

Ornate instruments of music,
of war: on stage and in the heart's timeless silos
imagine what they are upto.

4. Soloist

You are afraid she will teeter off the stage
and onto the lap of the front-row matron
crushing there a cellophaned bouquet.

In her motley single-piece costume
barefoot she is almost prancing
between conductor and concert-master.
The second movement's demonic goading
of soloist and ensemble
no doubt warrants her animation.
But she is in a frenzy and you are afraid
that something will go wrong.
Someone will come in late (she is
too fast for anything to happen early)
or one of her afflicted strings will break.
Is that the worst that can happen?
What then? Will everything end
in shocked silence? A requiem?
Just then – apropos of nothing –
the music halts. Her bow is held up trembling
the orchestra deflates and someone coughs.
She slowly lowers her hand. Flowers
are deferred to the next ending. You are
afraid that where a timely send-off
will only expose survivors to further attack
flowers can only do so much.

5. Double Basses

During the intermission you see
from your seat above the stage
five double basses supine
like beached whales or jumbo jets.

They are quite useless where they lie
but have lost none of the sheen
you noticed during the slow movement
when you peered over the balcony.

The bows in steady unison
drew up a message from the deeps.
Here was soulful death and here
a readiness to take to the skies

to air the hall-wide intelligence
that war can always be survived.

6. French Horn

You watch him from the beginning
the only one of his kind
sitting demurely in a row towards the back.

When he puts his gleaming instrument to his lips
you hear it distinct from the rest
or think you do.

You know his moment will arrive
in the fourth movement
when he must sound clear above the orchestra

raising the sun through a valley
dispersing the cowbell mist for a lone flute
abidingly to follow.

This you anticipate
yet it comes as always glowingly
it comes like the sun on devastated horizons.

7. Anchor

The percussionist at the very back
is not flamboyant-cool.
He will not set your heart pounding.
Nor does he look as if he wants to:
portly in his tux
his forehead buffed above the trim white beard
professorial behind his specs
he is mostly still
his instruments like those of combat
mostly unused.
Tubbily they surround the swivel chair
on which forearms crossed he sits.
Like the team anchor in a tug-of-war
his role is to be unmoved
as the music almost slips away.
Then out of nowhere
sticks appear in his pudgy hands.
He leans slightly forward.
In the nick of time
he reels the music in
only for it to be released from your grasp.
Little used but doing so much:
how cool is that.

8. Grand Piano

Standing in the rubble undestroyed
is a grand piano
grander for all that lies around.
The makings of an orchestra
are in pieces.

It was impertinence
to acquire instruments such as these
social climbing in a war-zone
whose children are a stone-throwing rabble
deadly each one.

David's time is gone.
Righteous stones are irrelevant
to laser directed shells and camouflaged tanks
furnished by giant financiers
before the concert.

Here a concert grand
stands within a smoke screen.
It was last tuned a few years ago.
You do not know what time there is:
play on.

Time In Four Nutshells

1. A Matter Of Time

Sooner or later it must be found out
though age can be deceptive.
The orange sun is so much older
than it appears.
Older than the red banner
that's prematurely ravaged
with having hit the wind all night.

Between banner and sun is a river
of indeterminate vintage.
Gliding towards it are two black birds
whose lifespan is being dissolved.

Between the pair of sooty boats
that time does not possess

a new shimmer is reaching for you
not for the first time
and not that it matters.

2. On Killing Time

Resist the urge to kill it.
It is more useful alive
and ticking. You can always

bear with more of it.

In pain and pleasure it feels
unlimited. All yours.
But it serves everyone.
It does not stop with you.

So kill it if you must
in a jealous rage and not
because of a yawn. Let time
heed you at the last.

3. Racing Against Time

Knowing you have to stay ahead
has given you second wind.

Time does not react when you go faster.
He eyes the crowd lining the track.

This throws them back. Why are they here?
They have placed illicit bets

on a showdown between time and will.
Their lives hinge on narrow victories.

But striving to win is not his style.
He comes metronomically

and goes. The intervals you time between

one lapping of him and the next

have begun to lengthen. His pulse
bloodless his breath stirs nothing.

4. Ahead Of time

You do not know the ends of time.
Death is untimely
even when it was the best alternative.

Something always remains to be said.
What that is you do not know
and the time for it is over.

The dead have done without
the confidences you did not reveal.
They are always ahead of time.

Watching The Match

We sit high in the floodlit stands.
The action looks small.
Huge screens give us a closer view.
Blood on turf glitters under lights.
Our brute sympathies
we say are with the underdog.
Our gesticulations are caught on screen
and alter nothing: this is
the time of the overdog.
We should switch allegiances.
Referees run along the sidelines
and blow their whistles.
This adds to the spill of red on green
the squelching of those who still play.
Some have lost heart: if it comes their way
they kick the ball to be rid of it.
Some kick themselves.
We stand and applaud
despite the wetness in our boots.
Attempt a Mexican wave.

Screenshot: Red And Green

A convoy of military trucks
is coming up the country lane.
The caption says they are on a flag march
to keep the peace between warring tribes.
Hanging out of the drivers' cabs are red flags.
Triangular red plates are fixed below one bonnet.

But the trucks are mostly dark green
almost black as if indelibly stained
by the shade of forests disappeared.
The tribes out in the open now
must fight each other to be first in line.
Here are trucks to keep the peace unstoppably.

The photo shows another green and red
unstoppable thing: resplendent
as it arches above that single file
is a gulmohar tree. Slightly out of focus
doing its thing exotically
until peace-keeping distends every road.

Screenshot: The Third

Prop it against the table lamp.
You have been avoiding it: now write.
Of this first: the bandages broad and white
that two of them wear around their heads.
So white: they mark the progeny of peace.
A third is beside the two
and all three are seated on a kind of bench.

One of the bandaged looks straight ahead.
He has a yellow patch on his cheek
and blotches of red on his grey sweatshirt.
His eyes are expressionless
but he has a get-me-if-you-can bearing
as if he feels the demands of enmity.
His hands are together on his lap.
He has been schooled in obedience:
he must be the eldest.

The other next to him is also in grey
and also has the red blotches
to emulate the older one his hero.
He has a smart design on the front
and a faux logo on his pants.
He is looking up at the camera
not pretending to be anything now.
His face has crumpled. He doesn't know
what he has done. He knows

nothing of true enmity. Forgive him.
Forgive him his dream of a flashy gun.

The third is being attended to
by a man in a mask and surgical gloves
kneeling in front to fix him
his watch bracelet catching a dull light.
The third non-bandaged being attended to:
a woman bending over him
is raising his face by the chin
her other hand on his shoulder
as the kneeling man does what he can.

Her face is shadowed. Veiled in black
Mary's negative from a cold Pietà
she is roused to do what she can
when it comes to flesh and blood. You cannot
know the expression in her eyes.

The third has a crater beside his eye
as if his cheek were the Little Prince's planet.
Why go there now? And where?
Why? His face is despairing
because humanity is too much for him.
The miracle of his appearance has gone.

Notre Dame

A cathedral burns.
Tears at the tears of one
who in dazed silence watches.

No helping tears for tears.
Not everything
has gone up in flames.

No stopping burns
for burns. No watching long
enough what this does

to homes this side that side
enough for tears to stop
burning.

The Balcony

Magic lanterns are up there
behind that balcony's potted forest.
In the daytime you knew it to be

a facade of designer lines and whitewash.
All that heavy greenness
spilling over the seventh floor

felt as if it were planted immovably
to prevent signals from getting out
or in. But look at it now

every gust a revelation
that the massed plants are powerless to resist.
A shell is being broken out of

bits of history being flung aside.
An opening on the walls of night
a directive flashed in code:

you will have to learn if it can be deciphered.
With the wind falling
there isn't much time for this. Already

stillness is taking hold.
The silent leaves are plastering the cracks.
The balcony is being gagged.

The Watchman

The watchman – that is to say the man
who mends watches –
does not look the part.
He looks to be the problem when times are awry.
He has a muscleman's shoulders
a politician's paunch
and a mafiosi's slur of speech.
His cubbyhole must cramp his style.
He does not look you in the eye
and he is careless of his sparse hair.

But nothing is careless
in what his hands are upto.
Beneath the glass attached to his eye
his stubby fingers
are doing things to things you cannot see.
The drawer his stomach grazes is half open
and he reaches in without looking
for the implement he needs
or for the bag of empty tags
to label watches with their people.
The pen has its place across the table
spares are in stacked boxes –
batteries, straps, protective glass, whatnot –
and alarm clocks line the shelves.

But no alarms
in this precisely congested space
that runs like the insides of a watch.
Things are kept as they should be
and here if anywhere
sits the boss of small things. In quiet
ready for you: he is the nub
when ticking needs to be set right.

Migraciones

in continuum Gloria Gervitz

She reveals that in her 60s
she was newly loved and fell in love
so she moved to be with him
across a tough border.
All her life had been on this side.

After the reading she speaks
wonderingly about the move.
But it should surprise no one
least of all herself. Frontiers
are her lifework.

All women she is all crossings.
She roams translated pages
with an orphan's freedom.
A hybrid past is in the present
dead women come alive

the market place is teeming
and sex is pleasurable
even without a partner.
All things naked and inviolate
are in the poem with you.

Skimming

My subject is War, and the pity of War.
The poetry is in the pity.
Wilfred Owen

"Politics makes for bad poetry"
you once thought to declare.
Was your subject poetry
or the fallout when power struts its hour
bestrewing the ground with half-eaten fruit?

Poetry is unembarrassed to find
some kinds of wasting beautiful.
It has its head down
as it scuffs its shoes on the shores
of what it does not know.
Questing for a smooth stone to skim
it is easy to ignore.

Politicking is that motorboat
slickly fitted out and gleaming
as it churns the rough water
its flag ablaze with information and intent
its wake turning the surface white.
It shows no sign of going under.
It races up and down and crosswise
leaves its mess spreading wherever it goes
so it is hard to ignore.

Once in a way you listen
to the lake as it is being skimmed.
You follow the diminishing hits
until the surface tension breaks
and a thing is lost to water.

You could have remarked that poetry
picks up residual stones to fling
in the interstices of war.

Paradise Flycatcher

All I have is a voice
W.H. Auden 'September 1, 1939'

Poetry makes nothing happen
W.H. Auden 'In memory of W.B. Yeats'

I

This is a tailorbird.
That is (listen!) a barbet.
This much you know from the App
that gives you names for the calls.

How little you know. Likewise
of people beyond their tags.
But in this universe
names become the markers

you settle on. They are
the "Ironic points of light"
that keep you dark: history's
beacons for time's discards.

Consigned with them if all
you have is a voice let birds

show you how to lift it
across the rubbish heap.

The earth receives its guests
as if they were all poets
whose embers touch the air
with barely happened voices.

II

Poetry makes things happen
at times. One evening a flicker:
a gliding upward a whiteness
against a mottled tree

up up in quick stages
the tail a streamer a bird
outdoing its brand. A wordless
question begins to form.

Relentless the windy rubbish
that follows after and spreads
malignantly. But know
that poetry's hand was raised.

A way of happening
more than a mouth: a stance
without the megaphones.
You cannot win the war

of shouting the other down.
Opinion smothers the cries
of sadness and of hope.
Poetry can hear it all.

Envoi

Birds cry out: listen.
Attentive voices range
where no one's loss is a win.

Listening is less
than a stance. With it the words
that land on water and rise

may cross the earth's frontiers.
Time does not stop them
because they echo the sea.

Your Room

for Karen Hesli and Jeff Welch

The room opens to trees in the sun
where the earth is threaded by a creek.
The room is open above the trees to a ridge
that caught the sun like the early bird
but shared it all the way down.
Now the oranges are full with it.

The room carries a river past trees
with stories to gather before they soften
too much. The trees are shadowed by birds
departing. One story is of a river
dammed where its first people rest.
They listen to rivers held all over the earth.

The room has heard the quiet resolve
of creatures that choose to die in rivers
upstream of dams. Their passage
is not forgotten here. This room
does not violate their stillness
nor rob the earth of pips delivered by birds.

The room has space for all our stories
as the ocean has for rivers and the trees
for oranges. Their tartness is in the sun
wherever rinds are hardening.
Listen for the calm wing-beat
that carries all the earth each morning.

Delivery

Your heart is idling after it churned
the river all day long.

Sea-birds keen above the estuary's
scattered shores. Direct

your ears to an overloaded boat
chugging through small channels

with assorted goods and tittle-tattle.
Unburdened it is renewed.

Acknowledgements

All of the poems in the first two sections of the book and a few in the third were written in Banaras, at the Rajghat centre of the Krishnamurti Foundation India. I am grateful to the community at Rajghat for being what it is: warm-hearted, creative and diverse; and, like the apparently unchanging river that the tree-filled campus overlooks, usually unhurried while being always on the move.

I gratefully acknowledge the editors of the following publications in which some of the poems have appeared:
Verseville - 'Waking' and 'Portrait'
Yapanchitra - 'Time In Four Nutshells'
Open Magazine - 'The Balcony' and 'Migraciones'

And my deepest gratitude to the team at Hachette for believing in this book and bringing it out. A special thanks to Thomas Abraham, whose irreverent response to some lines I produced many years ago was an early, if possibly unintended, signal to not be worshipful of the stuff one writes; and to Abhivyakti Singh: it would be hard to imagine a more engaged, discerning and empathetic poetry editor. Thanks too to Harshavardhan Behura for producing the wonderful line drawings that open each section of the book, and to Pia Alizé Hazarika for designing such an elegant cover.

Finally, I must mention how privileged I feel to have a section of Shammi Bannu Sharma's exquisite miniature grace the cover of the book.

Notes

Confluence (3. Moon)

"when kheer is placed on the roof"
A tradition during the Sharad Purnima that falls in September/October.

River Mornings (9. Ol' Man River)

A song from the musical *Show Boat*, made memorable by Paul Robeson's rendering of it. The song's refrain goes: "But ol' man river / He jes' keeps rollin' along!"

River Mornings (10. Hanamichi)

In the Japanese kabuki theatre, the hanamichi ("flower path") is a long platform that extends the stage through the audience.

"an act that ends like all the world"
cf. Shakespeare: "All the world's a stage" in *As You Like It*

"signifies something"
cf. Shakespeare: Life's "a tale / Told by an idiot, full of sound and fury, / Signifying nothing." (*Macbeth*)

Moonflower

There is such a thing as a moonflower (the tropical white morning glory) but the flower of this poem is imaginary.

Words In Season

"Season of mists and mellow fruitfulness" opens John Keats' 'To Autumn'.

A Poem For Lunch

The poem being read aloud is the third in Seamus Heaney's 'Clearances', a sonnet sequence that memorializes the poet's mother.

The Griper At The Gates Of Dawn

'The Piper at the Gates of Dawn' is the title of a lyrical chapter in Kenneth Grahame's children's novel *The Wind in the Willows*. (The title was used by Pink Floyd, the English rock band, for their first studio album.)

The final stanza makes reference to Diogenes the Greek philosopher, including an encounter, very likely apocryphal, with Alexander the Great, in which philosopher tells visiting king to stop blocking the sunlight.

Teens On Shravan Monday

During Shravan (July/August) devotees of Shiva perform special rituals on Mondays, including fasts from dawn to dusk.

Shedding

The epigraph is from Szymborska's luminous Nobel lecture in 1996. The full paragraph reads: "The world – whatever we might think when terrified by its vastness and our own impotence, or embittered by its indifference to individual suffering, of people, animals, and perhaps even plants, for why are we so sure that plants feel no pain; whatever we might think of its expanses pierced by the rays of stars surrounded by planets we've just begun to discover, planets already dead? still dead? we just don't know; whatever we might think of this measureless theater to which we've got reserved tickets, but tickets whose lifespan is laughably short, bounded as it is by two arbitrary dates; whatever else we might think of this world – it is astonishing."

Coconut Man

'Cocoanut Woman' is a Harry Belafonte song that begins:
"Coconut woman is calling out
And every day you can hear her shout...."

Concert (8. Grand Piano)

The poem draws on news reports of a grand piano that survived bombing attacks in Gaza, while several other musical instruments around it were destroyed.

For instance: https://www.bbc.com/news/articles/ce8151n1elno